The Loss of the
Lake Champlain Bridge

The Loss of the Lake Champlain Bridge

A Traveler's Story

Jean Arleen Breed

Jean Arleen Breed

Bloated Toe Publishing
Peru, New York 12972

Library of Congress Control Number 2011903240

ISBN: 978-0-9795741-7-7

Copies of this book may be purchased online at
The North Country Store
http://www.bloatedtoe.com/store/home.php

or

Visit Bloated Toe Enterprises website:
URL: www.bloatedtoe.com
Email sales@bloatedtoe.com

or

Write to:
Bloated Toe Enterprises
Box 324
Peru, NY 12972

Covers designed and created by Lawrence P. Gooley

Front Cover photo by Jean Arleen Breed
Back Cover photo by Francis L. Breed

Image on bottom of page 48 created by HNTB Corporation, and used with permission of the New York State Department of Transportation (NYSDOT)

Printed and bound by
Versa Press, Inc., 1465 Spring Bay Road, East Peoria, IL 61611-9788

Manufactured in the United States of America

For Todd and Sharon—the center of my heart

Contents

Tell Me a Story	1		Travel on with Hope	37
The Bridge	4		Henry and Louise	39
Our Choices	6		One Week Later	40
You Looked Back	9		Magic	41
The Beginning	10		Hum	42
Pieces	12		Aren't We Lucky	44
Before	13		Golden Gate	45
Everybody Brings Something	15		Let it Go	46
Move That Rock	16		Glass	47
Make a Ripple	17		Welcome	48
Bring Your Good Stuff	18		Wait	49
The Ti Ferry	24		Why?	51
The Travelers	25		And Still	52
You'll Never Know	26		Freedom	55
Tough It	27		Shine	56
Spin-Out	28		Echoes	57
Chaos	30		The Forts	59
Tractor-Trailers	31		Wander	60
Thanksgiving	32		Valley Thunder	62
Ben's Christmas	33		Goodbye, Dear Bridge	63
Happy New Year	35		The Journey	64
Valentine's Day	36		About the Author	67

Saint Christopher,

Patron Saint of Travelers,

please keep us safe.

Acknowledgments

This story began on October 16, 2009, when the Lake Champlain Bridge was permanently closed to all traffic. The bridge was located between Crown Point, New York and Chimney Point, Vermont. This was the only bridge for eighty miles. Now, to go from one side of the lake to the other—where the bridge had once stood—took two hours and a long, winding drive around the lake.

As I lived in New York and worked in Vermont—like over three thousand other people—I was faced with the daunting task of getting to work every day. Suddenly, all our lives changed and we were in a battle for the very existence of our way of life in the Champlain Valley.

As people started to gather together and mobilize in order to get a new bridge built where the old one had stood, I became friends with folks who came to be known as the Lake Champlain Bridge Coalition (LCBC).

During this horrible time, I wrote many poems to keep these people encouraged, and soon there were a few folks who said I should write a book about all of this. So, here is that book.

I thank Karen and Lorraine and the countless people from the Lake Champlain Bridge Coalition who helped us to keep this valley alive. They put it on the line and went to bat and got a new bridge for us, and I thank them from my heart. Without them, the life we knew would be gone from this valley.

New York Assemblywoman Teresa Sayward and Vermont Representative Diane Lanpher told me that my words were part of the history of what took place in the Champlain Valley during 2009 and 2010.

Everybody has their own story—this is mine. I hope you enjoy this little book and think of it every time you drive over a bridge.

Foreword

Why did I write this book?

So I would never forget what happened when one single bridge closed.

I never want to forget the impact this bridge closing had on thousands of people in the Champlain Valley. Lives changed, businesses struggled, and people were tested.

I never want to forget the courage and conviction of these people as I watched their businesses struggle to survive, their farms barely hang on, and the workers' commutes turn into a daily four-hour odyssey. This story tells about those people and what they did to defend their right to continue life as they knew it for the past eighty years. The bridge was built, a way of life was built around that bridge, and then—suddenly—that bridge was gone and our entire valley was impacted.

I never want to forget that two states were involved, and through it all we came to realize that there was one heart beating in this valley. We so relied on each other—jobs, businesses, farms, hospitals, colleges—for just everything that made up our day-to-day life was tied to that bridge, and we didn't realize it until the bridge was gone. The bridge was the link that held us all together, and without that vital link, we fell apart—but not for long. The heart and spirit of the people who live here came together to rally and fight to get a new bridge built—a daunting task in this economy.

I never want to forget driving a thousand miles a week to work; getting in that long, dark line of cars at 4:00 on snowy winter mornings; seeing the ferry crew get out the life jackets on the little ferry because the ice had such a grip on all of us; and spinning out my Jeep on icy roads. I always want to remember thanking God we didn't hit a telephone pole or tree and we could be here to drive another day.

I never want to forget the impact that one other bridge failing had on the people in Minneapolis. I know a man living there who went over the Interstate 35W Bridge, and ten minutes later it collapsed. Thirteen people died and 145 were injured. When the lawsuits were finally settled, one of the people injured said: "Justice would have been for this to never have happened and for our bodies to be whole, and our relationships to be whole." Victims said they would "trade every dollar we receive from this settlement for an original bridge that was built, maintained, and inspected properly."

This is our story about what happened during this time in the Champlain Valley. Maybe a hundred years from now another person who lives here will read my words and know what took place here during 2009, 2010, and 2011. They will know of the courage of the people who lived here then.

While some went out and fought the fight to get our bridge replaced, I had to go to work each day, so I did what I could. I wrote them all some poems and now, I write our story. Somebody once told me that I was a folksy writer and I'm happy to say, I am. Here is my folksy little book of photographs and poems. I hope you enjoy them. I just had to tell this story.

As I write these words, there are ninety-three bridges in New York State with a current safety rating at or below that given to the Lake Champlain Bridge prior to closure in October 2009.

Tell Me a Story

© Jean Arleen Breed

"Tell me a story," he used to say when it was time for bed.
"Tell me a story," he always said, this little sleepy head.

So I would tuck him in his bed and weave a magic tale.
Something with dragons and angel's wings – that would never fail.

He never made it to the end, but that was how it went.
Asleep with a smile on his little face, another story spent.

I didn't know then that was the start of telling all my stories.
But night after night I practiced on him, all about heroes' glories.

He liked the way the words all rhymed; they seemed to soothe his soul.
I just wanted him to go to sleep, a mother's nightly goal.

But he grew up and the stories stopped and rested for a while.
I didn't start to write again, till I started all those miles.

We needed a break those long, long days, so I told some stories of mine.
I wrote a few poems that summed it all up, and I kept getting in line.

During that winter of hell on earth, those stories got us through.
The stories helped, they pushed us on, and now the way is new.

So each time I think of writing my book, I'm not doing it for any glory.
I just want to tell you the magic parts – I want to tell you our story.

October 16, 2009

The Lake Champlain Bridge at Crown Point was permanently closed to all traffic. The story begins . . .

"New York has shortchanged highway and bridge projects by billions of dollars over nearly two decades, siphoning off funds set aside to pay for repairs and upgrades to cover other state expenses," New York Comptroller Thomas DiNapoli said Thursday. (*Press Republican*—Chris Carola)

My first letter to the editor . . .

Dear Editor:

The Bridge

If only the inspectors had done their jobs.
If only the bridge fund hadn't been robbed.

If only the preparedness man had written his plan.
If they were just honest, we wouldn't blow up that span.

While Lisa goes broke, George sleeps in his truck.
I don't see any committee or panel set up.

The people are trying, they are working so hard.
But where are the crooked ones, the ones to be charged?

I'm sure they get a paycheck, each one, every week.
Through all of this time, we don't hear them speak.

The Bridge

(continued)

All of this has been brushed under the rug.
Not one single person has been called a big thug.

But for the grace of God, nobody died.
The bridge could have collapsed with people inside.

We could have been killed, so many of us,
Because of the crooks who did this to us.

There is no end to the money available now.
It just pours right out, millions I vow.

To blow up the bridge, to build a new ferry.
Pay top price for everything, so much overtime it's scary.

Who do you think is paying for this?
For the money they're spending hand over fist.

Not the crooks, that's for sure, they're invisible now.
The businesses and the travelers foot another sacred cow.

We're trying to look forward, we go on every day.
But are we done with the past, can we just walk away?

I think there are questions still hanging out there.
We need to point fingers, we still need to care.

Sincerely,

Jean Arleen Breed
Crown Point, NY

October 17, 2009

So, how do we get to work now???

Our Choices

© Jean Arleen Breed

How do we get to our jobs right now – now that our bridge is gone?
We still need to go to work every day. That commute is going to be long!

How do the farmers go cut their corn on the other side of the lake?
How do they move their stock around? Just how long will that take?

How are the businesses going to survive? Their business is now cut in half.
Every road now ends at the lake; we can't get across or get back.

What about folks who are sick and need care? The hospital is now far away.
What about the ones who go to school over there? Is their choice to just move there
and stay?

Do we drive around the lake every day? That's a thousand miles a week!
Ride on the bus and then take a ferry? This path is indeed looking bleak!

Get up at 3:00 and get in that line and do the same thing again after work?
Day after day we do the same thing, and before long, just everything hurts.

Winter is coming and with it the snow and the roads get bad around here.
But we have to keep going, we need that paycheck, those benefits we have are so
dear.

What used to take thirty minutes each way has now turned into four hours.
Two in the morning and two after work, we need help here from some higher
powers.

Our Choices
(continued)

*Help soon comes in the form of good folks who gather together to be heard.
God bless those souls, they arrived just in time, and they came with their magical
words.*

Lake Champlain Bridge Coalition rally in Montpelier, Vermont (photos courtesy of LCBC)

October 2009

The Lake Champlain Bridge Coalition (LCBC)—a grassroots group of business owners, concerned citizens and civic leaders from New York and Vermont—focused on restoring travel and commerce along the Lake Champlain Bridge Corridor, vowing to not let the nightmare we have been through happen to another community. They have seen firsthand what can happen when our infrastructure fails.

Detours of ninety-five miles were now seen by corridor travelers whose commute times have increased by at least four hours a day for New York residents traveling to Vermont for employment.

Without this organization, there would not be a new bridge under construction.

Lake Champlain Bridge Coalition members on their way to a rally held in Albany, New York (photo courtesy of LCBC)

You Looked Back

I looked at all those smiling faces that shone right there today.
I was so happy to see all of you that I just have to say . . .

I got to see how courage worked when everything was bad.
You didn't just sit there and shed a tear, you tried with all you had!

Not only did you fight this war but you looked back to see
If there were others who might need some help – other folks like me.

Even when you met the worst you just kept going on.
You didn't let the message stop when our old bridge was gone.

From day to day and week to week and even all those months;
You kept your message in the news and never stopped this once.

When others threw their worst at you that seemed to make you strong.
You did the things that made the difference and just kept going on.

So my hat's off to everyone who made this group so good.
You didn't quit, you kept on going, and I just knew you would.

So smile those smiles and one day soon we all can cross that span.
Because you looked back and helped us out and gave us all a hand.

The Beginning

© Jean Arleen Breed

Together there's strength and you knew that right off so together you went into this fight.
Just humble folks who had lost their bridge and now had to do what was right.

You took the battle right to the places where they could hear your voice.
If we were to survive in this little valley, you really had no choice.

You just kept going; you spent the time and together you fought this war.
You started as strangers who gathered their courage and then you fought some more.

Like so many people who all lived in this valley, you made up a formidable line.
You worked so hard for so many years; you had been here all this time.

There was no way you would just turn your back and walk away from your home.
You gathered together and helped each other — no one went it alone.

So blessings on this group right here who battled for all of us.
They were the ones who stood for us all — they did it "Just because."

The good guys heard your message and came to see us and they brought money with them . . . blessings.

LCBC members with New York Governor David Paterson and Vermont Governor James Douglas (photo courtesy of LCBC)

They had fought so long and hard, it seemed only right they start the new bridge with their own hands. From left to right: Crystal Stoddard, Vermont Representative Diane Lanpher, LCBC members Karen Hennessey and Lorraine Franklin (photo courtesy of LCBC).

Pieces

Pick up all those precious pieces and see if they still fit;
One, then two, then all the rest that took a horrid hit.

Try to place them in their spot, be gentle with them all.
They had a tough time just like us, they hit against the wall.

But look at them, they all slide in and settle without a sound.
They join together just like us, their lives are finally found.

With help and hope and tears the pieces start to look so whole.
What once was broken and in shreds, is not this empty hole.

How did it happen that it got fixed; how did this occur?
With people who stepped up and fought the fight and caused a joyful stir.

They picked it up, they carried it, and they knew the magic words.
They joined together and took in strays, the ones who had been hurt.

The fight was long, the battle hard, the days just seemed so tough.
But in the end, they won the war, their courage was enough.

Blessings on every single person who stands up for what they believe in . . .

Before

© Jean Arleen Breed

What can I say to all of you that comes straight from my heart?
What can I do to find the words, where is the place to start?

I traveled on alone at first; I just couldn't ride that bus.
Before Colette, before the group, I wandered in the dusk.

The miles were long, the days were dark, and the roads were hell on wheels.
I force myself to go each day, no matter how it feels.

Then a message came one day. It shone right in my eyes.
This group of people took me in and then Colette arrives.

The drive still came each morn and night; the roads still were not kind.
But now I have so much to help keep all this off my mind.

Karen wrote the heartfelt words, she said it all just right.
Her pain was there right on the page; she fought the valiant fight.

Lorraine – so brave, was right out there, she said the magic words.
To let the world know all the truth, she talked until they heard.

Joe and Cindy showed the light, they let us stop each day.
We took so much more than food with us when we went on our way.

Barb let us know what's going on, the stuff we needed then.
She always knew and shared with us so we wouldn't have to fend.

Lisa kept a watch for us, to let us know the facts.
Was work going on or not that day? She kept us all on track.

Before

(continued)

Robin took the pictures then, to let us see the deal.
That was so good; we got to know how far they built the steel.

Marion and Lauri and Crystal sent me words that I needed to hear.
They cheered me up, they helped me so, and they eased my daily fear.

Janet sent me messages that made me smile sometimes.
One tough lady, Janet is, she won't stand still for crimes.

Rich was so true to all that's right, he already knew this war.
He cheered us on and helped us out, and showed us the right door.

Darwin gave us all a break; he offered to share what he had.
We stopped sometimes to fill the tank, but he didn't know we had.

Andy cheered us when we let the world know of our plight.
He knew we had to say we wouldn't drop this horrid fight.

George kept going no matter what; he drove the most of any.
Sometimes he slept in his truck at night; George paid more than many.

I know that others helped me, too; I thank you all for that.
I pray we all go forward now; we don't want to go back.

I made it through this time of hell with help from everyone.
Before I knew this group of angels, my fight would not be won.

Thank you for the help, my friends, thank you for the time.
Thank you for the messages, soon I won't ever have to sign . . .

Jean Arleen Breed – Traveler – 2009/2010

Everybody Brings Something

© Jean Arleen Breed

Every single person adds something to this world.
We all bring color to the palette of this enchanting mural.

The swirls are made by everyone, they blend right in together.
No matter where we each come from, we need this place forever.

For this place is our home right here and will be till the end of time.
If you take care of your part now, I'll take care of mine.

I'll write a poem that has some words to let us see what's right.
You can do the other part; you might just have to fight.

The ones before and those before and the two who started out;
Had a garden in this world and it was great, no doubt?

They got sent out, they had to leave, but we can't leave our place.
So we all need to bring our piece so we don't lose our grace.

So – write and paint and sculpt and pray and do your very best.
So when the questions are put to us, we will pass that test.

One by one our pieces fit and then the world is saved.
Without each one, there is no hope; we'd lose the world He gave.

Move That Rock

© *Jean Arleen Breed*

Did I move that rock a bit; did I do my share?
While I was here on this good earth, did I really care?

Each one of us should move a rock and do something good for all.
We need to keep it moving on, or else the earth will fall.

We don't have to move it much, not by a whole lot.
All we have to do is try, give it all we've got.

You might not know your rock is there, it might just take some time.
It could be years before you say, "Yes, this one is mine!"

"This is what I have to do; my share is just right here."
Help somebody out today, don't be ruled by fear.

The rock will move when kind hearts give just something to help out.
You might not see it budge at all; but it will move no doubt.

Mine was heavy, so is yours, but giving helps a lot.
When I gave some of my heart, it moved from that one spot.

So keep a lookout for your rock; you'll know it when it comes.
You'll recognize what you can do to make the angels hum.

Your rock will be a lot for you, but not more than you can do.
Keep on going and it will move just like He always knew.

Make a Ripple

Did you make a ripple as you went through your days?
Did you stir the waters some with some of your own ways?

Were you quiet, meek, and still or did you make a fuss?
Was your life about being quiet or did you learn to cuss?

Will you leave some beauty behind, something that you did?
Will people long remember you, from the time you were a kid?

Go ahead and use your talent, use your God-given skills.
So what if it isn't perfect now? Just go up the hills!

I dive right in and make a splash and sometimes make a mess.
I so need to make my ripple, I can't take anything less.

I may never publish my book, but at least I gave it a try.
I'm sure most people would shake their head and simply ask me "Why?"

"Just because" is reason enough, it's good enough for me.
So make your ripple and enjoy the ride, let the world just see.

Bring Your Good Stuff

© Jean Arleen Breed

Bring your good stuff when you come for you will need it all!
No whimpers, sighs, or sad excuses to hang up on the wall.

The time is here, the stage is set, the curtains going up.
Before the lights have all been dimmed, be sure to fill your cup.

Bring your list of all you did, the good deeds and the bad.
You're going to be reviewed in here; I hope your results aren't sad.

Did you live a life of joy? Did you give some love?
What kind of person were you here? We watched you from above!

The times when you were truly tested, how did you make it through?
Did strength come out and help you then and did you start anew?

Was your heart big enough to share with all the rest?
Could you see the lonely ones? The ones we truly blessed?

Did you spend your precious days all wrapped up in yourself?
Did the Bible just sit there getting dusty on that shelf?

What's the best you ever did? Tell us all about it.
Even one thing you can recall, we would never doubt it.

So, come on in and bring your stuff, I hope it all adds up.
For this place is so magical, it will always fill your cup.

November 2009

More good guys arrive . . .

Rich Couch, MPA, Director of Advocacy, the Crisis Program

Rich gave the people of the Lake Champlain Bridge Coalition such good information and encouragement. They now knew that ninety-three bridges in New York State had a current safety rating at or below that given to the Lake Champlain Bridge prior to closure in October. Rich was a candle in this long, dark winter. His mission was advocating for New York State's roads and bridges.

Our local representatives—from New York and Vermont—became involved, battling long and hard to secure a new bridge. Thank you for understanding what we were going through and joining in this effort.

The Governors of New York and Vermont both became champions in this fight. Visiting the people of the Champlain Valley, they brought encouragement and funds to build a new bridge. This will long be remembered.

My hat is off to all of the people who took time to write Letters to the Editor. Your words were eloquent and needed. A day when there was a letter in the paper was a good day in the valley.

Lohr McKinstry (*Press Republican*), Fred Herbst (*Times of Ti*), Katie Zezima (*New York Times*), John Flowers (*Addison Independent*) and many other news folks helped so much with their stories. A hundred thanks to these kind souls who kept our battle in the news. Thank you to every single person who published my Letters to the Editor.

Unfortunately, the bad guys (or disinterested guys) arrived, too . . .

Paul Sands (from WPTZ television station in Plattsburgh) gave his opinion (and he was certainly entitled to do that): "Do the people in our valley really need a new bridge at Crown Point or should a new bridge be built elsewhere?" That's kicking us when we were down, Paul!

Thousands of people were struggling to drive four hours a day to keep their jobs; our businesses were down 70 percent; the lakeshore farmers were right on the edge of losing their farms; and some folks were even taking drastic measures like rowing across the lake to get to work—*and you wonder if we need a new bridge*? Yes, we do need a new bridge—that's my opinion, Paul.

Letters were written to the chairs of the Transportation Committee in both the State Assembly and the State Senate in Albany. As chairs of the Transportation Committee in each house, both have input into transportation.

Hon. Martin Malavé Dilan and Hon. David Gantt—I'm still waiting for a reply to the letters I sent to you both on January 15, 2010. Hello, hello—are you there? We're still here and we need help. I would have been happy to get even a form letter—anything. I can just picture my two letters and *A Traveler's Story* pitched in the nearest wastebasket. I hope, at least, you recycled it . . .

January 15, 2010

Hon. Martin Malavé Dilan, Chair   Hon. David Gantt, Chair
NYS Senate Transportation Committee   NYS Assembly Transportation Committee
Room 811 – Legislative Office Building   Room 830 – Legislative Office Building
Albany, NY 12247   Albany, NY 12248

Dear Hon. Martin Malavé Dilan and Hon. David Gantt:

I am forwarding this story so that others will realize they could be in the same danger that we were—driving on an unsafe bridge. I don't want to keep quiet and just let others go through what we are so I hope this letter will help somebody to avoid a tragedy of a bridge falling down. I could not stand to see any lives lost so I'm speaking up.

We must fund our infrastructure in New York and not let anyone raid that fund for other purposes than roads and bridges, AND those bridges must be properly inspected.

I thank you from my heart . . .

Jean Arleen Breed—Traveler—2009/2010

Enclosure: Day 90 and Counting—*A Traveler's Story*

Day 90 and Counting—*A Traveler's Story*

If the bridge in your area was to be condemned and closed, what would you do? Think it couldn't happen to you? I thought the same thing, and this is my story . . .

Since the Lake Champlain Bridge was condemned on October 16, 2009, thousands of people have struggled to commute from state to state to keep their jobs. We are known as the Travelers, and we travel by ferry, boat, bus, and car. Fourteen-hour days are normal now, paying huge chunks for gas is normal, getting up at 3:00 is normal, seldom seeing our families is normal, and seeing our businesses close is normal now. We have few traces of the life we used to know!

It's like a marathon, and after ninety days, everything hurts. We are totally tired out but we have to keep going.

Our businesses are suffering so; yet they have offered us beds, food, gas, and encouragement—blessings on those people! Though others have kicked us while we were down and wanted to take away our bridge forever, our businesses all offered us a hand and we will never forget their good hearts. Some of them have worked so hard for thirty years to build up their business only to watch it melt away these last ninety days.

We pray for the day the new ferry gets going and think of the workers who are building it! Blessings on them!

We talk of bridges across New York and Vermont and know there are bridges out there that are ready to collapse.

We agree we will never go over a bridge again and take it for granted that it is safe, no matter what the experts say!

After work, the Travelers don't talk much; everybody is tired and we just want the two-hour trip to go by and get home and hug the people we love and get ready for tomorrow so we can do it all again—ninety days and counting.

It is too late for us, but not too late for your community. Speak out—ask questions. Don't let yourself become one of the Travelers!

Jean Arleen Breed—Traveler—2009/2010 . . . Crown Point, NY

November 14, 2009

Dear Editor:

During this difficult time, when thousands of people have had their lives so impacted by the closing of the Crown Point Bridge, I would like to publicly thank the people who are associated with the Ticonderoga ferry.

You have all gone out of your way to provide not only an essential service, but have done it with genuine concern and understanding for folks who have to travel from state to state to work at their jobs.

You gave us all a price break; you started operating the ferry at 5:30 a.m. so we could all get to work on time; you told us to have a good day; and you promised to be there to take us back home at night. You were indeed a welcome light in the midst of all this darkness.

Bravo to each of you. If there is any award for the business with the biggest heart, you will win hands down.

On behalf of myself and all the people in that long line of cars waiting in the dark at 4:00 every morning, thank you so much. We will never forget all you did for us.

Jean Arleen Breed
Crown Point, NY

Due to heavy ice and insurance concerns, the Ticonderoga ferry closed for the season on December 31, 2009.

On January 1, 2010, hundreds of people started the long drive around the lake every day. To get to work, many drove over a thousand miles a week. These people came to be known as the Travelers.

Some rowed a boat across the lake until the ice was too thick. Some slept in their trucks at night to go to work the next morning. Some took a bus, then took a ferry, and then drove the rest of the way to work. Some drove, then rode across the lake in a boat, and then took another bus to get to work.

Any semblance of the life we knew was gone . . .

The Ti ferry before winter. Though it's a tiny craft, thousands of people got in line to use it (photo courtesy of Francis Breed).

The Ti Ferry

© Jean Arleen Breed

"The ferry's coming," I heard her say, so I got in my car.
We needed to get across the lake and the drive was just too far.

Our poor bridge had been blown up, but the lake was still right there.
We all needed to get to work but now it just wasn't fair.

We had to get up by three o'clock to go get in line by four.
It was so cold waiting in the car; we put blankets by the door.

That long, long line of cars in the dark just about broke my heart.
All those people just trying to survive and that was the horrible part.

The winter was long and cold that year, the roads were icy and wet.
They were building a new ferry landing but it wasn't ready yet.

So the little ferry kept going on, though ice and waves rattled us.
Only twenty cars could go at a time and there were thousands of us.

Just before Christmas we got out of our cars and hugged each other in peace.
That morning was dark and the wind just howled, but we had each other, at least.

One day we thought the ferry was done, they got out all the life jackets.
We all said a prayer and the ice finally gave; it crashed to the lake with a racket.

Finally the ferry couldn't go any more, their insurance said, " . . . enough."
We all thanked them so, those brave, brave people; they went when the going was tough.

So if you see a ferry on a lake one day, thank them for taking you across.
During our crisis, when the chips were down, without them we would be lost.

24

January 2010

The Travelers

No snowplows for the travelers today; but that's ok, we found our own way.

Our journey continues, our saga goes on, we travel and travel through darkness and dawn.

There were other travelers so long ago, on this wondrous journey we all came to know.

They followed a star, it shone so bright. They followed its path and knew they were right.

Their journey was hard, it took a long time, but they knew in their hearts to follow that shine.

At last those three travelers beheld such a sight; a miracle before them that cold winter night.

He lay in a manger. He was at peace. He knew those three travelers who dropped to their knees.

And just for that moment the world was so calm. Just for that moment no one traveled on.

So we will keep traveling and maybe one day – our journey will end, we can only pray.

You'll Never Know

© Jean Arleen Breed

Every single winter day we drove to work in the dark.
We left home each day at 4:00 and that wasn't the hardest part.

The drive was so long, two hours each way as we watched the months roll by.
Thousands of people in a long, winding line, each one was just asking, "Why?"

The dark and cold, the icy roads, the tractor-trailers, and us.
We drove every day just to get to our jobs and tried not to make a big fuss.

Just before Christmas we noticed something wonderful, something new by the road each day.
All those good people had put up some lights and those lights helped to show us the way.

Christmas trees that were beautifully decorated began to appear near the road.
Every day when we looked at them it seemed to ease our load.

From Shoreham, where we got off the ferry, to Bridport, and points going north.
We all enjoyed those lights every day; I can't tell you what they were worth.

It didn't seem like we were quite so alone, there were good people that lived in those homes.
They took the time to get ready for Christmas and the goodness of those folks just shone.

I had to just thank you for all that you did even though you didn't know we were there.
All those small towns, all those warm lights, showed just how much you could care.

You'll Never Know
(continued)

So the next time you decorate when Christmas is coming I hope you remember this poem.
You may never know who will be touched by your lights, whose way your lights safely guide home.

Tough It

© Jean Arleen Breed

Some take the bus, but I can't do that.
The bus makes me sick and that is a fact.

So I drive around the lake every day.
Colette rides with me, she goes the same way.

She has a great accent, this French friend of mine.
She works where I do and we have a good time.

She talks to me when we commute in the dark.
Day after day we have to embark.

Sometimes it's hard to drive in the snow.
But we just have to keep going where we have to go.

We both have a job that we are trying to keep.
Each day we keep going when we would so rather sleep.

We get up at three and get home about five.
Fourteen hours a day in this new bridgeless life.

Tough It
(continued)

Now we have treats, something fresh every day.
Cindy gives us cinnamon rolls to take on our way.

Sometimes I get scared; it's dark and it's cold.
But Colette tells me something and it's something I hold.

She gets in the car and just before we leave,
Colette tells me this, and now I believe.

"Jean, we just have to tough it," she says every day.
She tells me that sentence before we pull away.

I cling to those words; yes, we have to be tough.
Because Colette has such faith, the road isn't so rough.

So we will keep going till help finally arrives.
Two travelers together and we will survive.

Spin-Out

© Jean Arleen Breed

There came one day – one day like so many, when everything changed for me.
Up to that time, I had just driven along, with my caravan for company.

This one morning, when the roads seemed fine, I couldn't see anything wrong.
We were chattering together, driving to work, when suddenly we skidded along.

Spin-Out
(continued)

We went in a circle and then went toward a ditch; we both had no time to scream.
I cranked on the wheel, I did what I could, then this all seemed like a dream.

Out of control, that's what we were, and then suddenly the Jeep seemed to crash.
It was quiet for a minute, we both looked around, but we couldn't see anything smashed.

I thought I could hear a tractor-trailer that was coming up over the hill.
We had to get out of that ditch right away or else we would both be there still.

I put it in reverse and said a small prayer and that Jeep backed out of the snow.
It didn't look like we had hit anything, but we still had a long way to go.

I drove up the road and the Jeep sounded fine, I pulled over and stopped when I could.
I looked at the tires and looked at the back and looked at the snow-covered hood.

The gauges were fine, all seemed to be good, so we drove all the rest of the way.
It wasn't until I had my first cup of tea that my hands started to shake some that day.

That night after work, we looked for our skid, but couldn't see our tracks anywhere.
I know I drove slowly for days after that, each day I took such special care.

We were lucky that time; we both lived to tell about our spin-out on the ice.
Never again did I drive very fast, people passed me, then passed me twice.

Please replace our old bridge so we don't have this drive, this drive is just such a long way.
That is my story about my spin on the ice, just one more bad memory that will stay.

Chaos

© Jean Arleen Breed

I thought that I was trapped in hell; it seemed that way sometimes.
Drive and drive and drive some more and then just get in lines.

The roads were bad, the miles were long, and the end was not in sight.
I worked all day and drove for hours and collapsed in bed at night.

I wasn't alone on this endless trek; there were thousands like me out there.
We just tried to keep our paycheck going, but we didn't really get anywhere.

The price of gas, the toll of travel, the cold and dark went on.
But then one day I realized just how I had been wrong.

I looked up at the sky one morning as I waited for the ferry to come.
When did I last see stars come out or greet the morning sun?

I needed to restore some order to my world. I needed some peace in my heart.
I vowed to do better and withstand this chaos and then I made a new start.

Here I was surrounded by beauty and I couldn't even see it before.
I should be grateful for all that I had and I should stop asking for more.

This time would end and life would resume and wasn't that enough after all?
This wasn't a fraction of what troubles can be; this was a temporary fall.

Then it got easier, I wasn't so stressed. I let all the days just roll by.
I wrote lots of poems and that kept me going and finally I quit asking, "Why?"

Tractor-Trailers

That long, long drive went on each day but I was never alone.
Thousands of folks were out there too, their taillights bravely shone.

A caravan of trucks lead the way and sometimes they plowed the roads.
I can't imagine all that weight or hauling those heavy loads.

Someone's dad was driving that truck and someone's son was too.
I cheered for them to make it home whenever they finished their route.

That UPS truck had a lady driving and she told me her daughter was home.
She was late getting back as the roads were so bad and she worried her girl
was alone.

It was always dark when I drove both ways so I got to see all their lights.
Some of those trucks looked like magical things. They made our darkness bright.

I watched them as they filled their tanks. I can't imagine what that cost!
They were out in the cold just like us. I hope they never got lost.

So now every time I see a big truck, I say a prayer for them.
Let all of them be safe today; let their drive just end.

We traveled on through Thanksgiving, Christmas, New Year's Day, and Valentine's Day.

No matter what, we kept on traveling.

Thanksgiving

© Jean Arleen Breed

Add up all the things we have and bow our heads in thanks.
Count the things that aren't just things and see just where we rank.

The air is clean, the trees are lush, and the fish are in our streams.
We can walk wherever we want and dream our hopeful dreams.

The freedom is so big right here; we're blessed with the brave ones.
The ones who go and make it last and fight when battle comes.

We can say just what we think and gather where we want.
We can pray in our own place and we can fish and hunt.

There's those who come and rescue us and keep us safe at night.
They put their own lives on the line to make sure ours is right.

The schools are here for all the kids, to teach them what they need.
Those teachers are the blessed ones to teach the kids to read.

The library is in every town, such treasures on those shelves.
We can read these wonderful books or write one for ourselves.

There's so much to be thankful for, this country fills our cup.
We are so blessed, when we look around and then just add it up.

Ben's Christmas

© Jean Arleen Breed

This is the story of an angel named Ben.
It's a story of Christmas and goodwill to men.

Ben was in trouble, he might have to leave.
He had just one last chance, to make Michael believe.

Ben was sent on a mission to help people below.
Come back with a report soon or else you will go!

Ben ran to the village, he looked at the town.
He could see he was needed, he started to frown.

There were things to be done, things to set right.
Ben rolled up his wings and he started that night.

First, get rid of all hunger, get rid of all fear.
Ben fixed that quickly, with barely a tear.

The children should learn; they should know how to read.
Ben left them a big book full of good deeds.

Make the bombs stop, conquer the disease.
"Let there be peace." Ben prayed on his knees.

Some kids needed a good home, Ben saw their plight.
With love in his heart, Ben made that right.

He looked for the manger, surely they must have one!
He found it on the chapel porch, right there in the sun.

Ben's Christmas
(continued)

Did they give to charity? Did they help others out?
When Ben knew that answer, he gave up a shout.

When times got tough there, what did these people do?
They helped out each other. Ben cried when he knew.

This town had some churches, a restaurant, and some stores.
Ben could see people working, near the lake, on the shores.

It had far more than buildings; it had a kind, gentle heart.
Ben recognized the angels, they all played a part.

They worked and they played and they gathered in prayer.
People like these can't be found everywhere.

Ben saw so much kindness; it went straight to his heart.
These people all know love, they each play a part.

The way that they lived there, so touched his soul.
Ben knew in that instant, he could get to his goal.

There, Ben was all finished, he made his report.
These people were so good, they just needed support.

Now they're at peace and so is dear Ben.
He's back in the garden, where it all began.

Happy New Year

© Jean Arleen Breed

As quietly as gentle words settle in a book,
Another year comes to call; we all can have a look.

What's in store for all of us? What does this year hold?
We've waged a war and won one battle, but the future is untold.

A brand new start for everyone, we all get an equal chance.
Don't think about what went before, don't give a backward glance.

For we can't change what came before, it's done and we go on,
Just take the day in front of us, and pray it will be calm.

Close your eyes and just imagine how this year will play out.
Our lives will change, for good this time, of that I have no doubt!

The freedom that we all imagine is coming week by week.
I hear the joy in hopeful voices every time they speak.

A hug from a friend and a New Year's greeting all came to me today.
She seemed so happy just to talk a minute and then went on her way.

The valley is in a waiting mode but it's starting to tilt toward glad.
Never will we take for granted all the freedom we had!

To once again just go someplace and come back when it's time.
To be able to plan and not consider how long we'll be waiting in line.

Our days of wasting our hours to get there are slowly ticking away.
I know I'll go on a drive that day no matter what they say!

So just look forward and think about it – it will almost bring a tear.
Once again we will have our lives and a blessed, brand New Year.

Valentine's Day

© Jean Arleen Breed

I've reached deep down to the bottom of my heart
To find enough courage to make a new start.

There's a piece missing there where joy had once stood.
A tiny crack, too, for when life was so good.

It's trying to mend, it just needs some time.
That nick in the side will one day be fine.

The bruise from the years is fading a bit.
One day before long it will look like it's fit.

It doesn't skip beats, like when this began;
Mostly it's steady, just a bump now and then.

It didn't escape without a few good-sized breaks.
But ever so slowly I do what it takes.

The heart is now mending with hardly a tear.
I thought there was damage but nothing to fear.

Each day it gets better, each day helps a lot.
This heart has withstood the battle I fought.

I've come a long way, a long way from the start.
I will find peace way down deep in my heart.

Travel on with Hope

© Jean Arleen Breed

Hope – a fragile wish my heart just made, so soft, so deep inside.
It struggled so to find a place it didn't have to hide.

I felt it when this gentle one arrived to warm my soul.
I didn't know just what it was or couldn't guess the goal.

It knew that others came before, but could not find a place.
But others knew this one would come; they left a path to trace.

The journey was so hard at first; it was uphill all along.
Doubt and fear both came to call, but this one was so strong.

It gathered prayers along the way, the angels blessed this one.
They knew it had to travel on if victory would be won.

Time and time and time again, it thought that all was lost.
But this blessed little grain of hope just knew the final cost.

If hope was gone and sorrow won, then every light went out.
It wouldn't give up no matter what, it never had one doubt.

Slowly, with its tiny light, the hope crept in my soul.
Slowly, I could feel it grow and I could see the goal.

Together, hope and I began to feel so glad inside.
Together, we began to know it wouldn't have to hide.

A few first steps, a day or two, and I knew it was there to stay.
I thank the angels who blessed this hope and had the strength to pray.

Now I can feel this joy inside that helps me so to cope.
I know its name, I feel its warmth, and I travel on with hope.

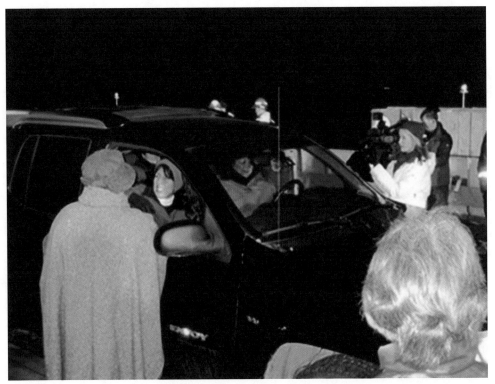

On February 1, 2010, two ferries from the Lake Champlain Transportation Company started operating where the bridge had been. They were free to the public and operated twenty-four hours a day. These boats were a blessing for all of us in the valley. No more four-hour commutes every day! Pictured above are Karen Hennessey and Lorraine Franklin on the first trip of the new Lake Champlain Transportation Company ferry (photo courtesy of LCBC).

Henry and Louise

We have a new ferry and it's a big deal.
Two ferry landings made of concrete and steel.

So many machines that clang and they bang.
We have enough workers to make up a gang.

There are two huge cranes that soar up in the air.
Barges are there – I think there's a pair.

I add to the racket with my studded snow tires.
Then Henry strolled by in his winter attire.

He and Louise were selecting a place
Where they could watch all the fuss with a smile on their face.

Our lack of two wings made us spend all this money.
Henry and Louise thought the whole thing was funny.

"Just look at all that," Louise said to her mate.
"I feel sorry for them, for this is their fate."

They're just people, after all, they bang and they fuss.
God in his wisdom gave the good stuff to us.

Henry stretched out his wings, a magnificent sight.
He strutted around in the glow of the light.

Louise said to Henry, "Quit showing off.
"Those poor things have no wings and that must be tough."

So when we get so puffed up with all our big bucks.
Think of Henry and Louise and be humbled by ducks.

One Week Later

© *Jean Arleen Breed*

The blessing has finally settled in my soul.
The ferry is staying, we reached our first goal!

It's so easy to get here now every day.
Just forty minutes, and that is one way.

I don't have to drive way down to Whitehall.
No more Benson Landing or very close calls.

No two-hour trips when I get up each day.
My home and my family aren't so far away.

I can stop at the store on my way here or back.
I can buy a few groceries and that is a fact.

I saved a hundred dollars last week on gas.
Now I only fill up once, not like the past.

I have evenings again; I can stay up past eight.
I can go for a walk or talk to my mate.

Four hours a day have been given to me.
I don't rush round in circles or drive like a thief.

I just get on a ferry and in five minutes flat,
I'm across that good lake and at night I go back.

"Whew!" – is all I can say at this point in time.
I thank you the dear people, you fixed us up fine.

I send you a hug and say thank you a lot.
You all worked so hard to get what we've got.

Magic

© Jean Arleen Breed

The new ferry has been here for two weeks now.
I've ridden on that ferry, from the stern to the bow.

This morning I realized how wonderful it is.
Not to just ride on the ferry, but to experience all this.

I'm not driving to work, I'm spending some time.
Looking at the wonders all around me I find.

The moon is so brilliant, just hanging in air.
The ducks and the geese keep us company there.

For centuries all this has been right there to see.
But my eyes weren't ready for the magic before me.

We had to be stopped in our rush to get there;
To just look around at all we have here.

When would I ever get a chance to do this?
Ride right on the lake, I tell you, it's bliss!

I finally realized just how lucky I am.
To be able to experience God's wonderful plan.

He has to just stop us, it took all of this.
To be able to see what our eyes had just missed.

So if this was the purpose of what we've been through,
To help us get focused on what we should do.

Then my heart is so grateful, I'll quit calling it tragic.
For within all of this, I have found all the magic.

Hum

A fifty-mile commute used to be so long;
Now that drive is nothing, now that I'm strong.

The snow and the sleet would have tested my nerves.
Now I sing with the radio, I cruise around curves.

The dark and the cold would have put me to whining.
So what if it's dark? Inside, the sun's shining!

Ride across the lake in the cold and the ice!
That would have been crazy, now I don't think twice.

Get in line every day and wait a short time.
I would have been grumpy, now I'm Mary Sunshine.

My home and my family used to be so far away.
Now, in a few minutes, I can be home to stay.

The planet has turned itself ever so slightly.
Now blessings are back and I praise it nightly.

Miles and time and stress have all gone.
Now life's almost normal where it really belongs.

I'm thankful, I'm glad, and I know we are blessed.
We are halfway through with this horrible mess.

We can watch a new friend come into that place
Where our gracious old lady used to show us her face.

So – take a deep breath, look how far we've come.
As for this happy camper, I'll just sit here and hum.

On October 16, 2010, there was a gathering of people to note the one-year anniversary of the closing of the Champlain Bridge.

October 16, 2010 Community Gathering

AGENDA

Note: The Cumberland Head and Grand Isle Ferries will "salute" the Old Bridge at 1:25 p.m. to signal the start of our program. Thank you, Lake Champlain Transportation.

☐ Welcome on behalf of the Lake Champlain Bridge Coalition (LCBC)— Karen Hennessy

☐ Invocation—Rev. David Hirtle, First Congregational Church, Crown Point

☐ Poem by Jean A. Breed: "Aren't We Lucky"

☐ Speakers:
- Lorraine Franklin, LCBC
- Lisa Cloutier, LCBC
- Barb Brassard, LCBC
- Rich Couch, MPA, Director of Advocacy, The Crisis Program
- Representative Diane Lanpher, VT
- Assemblywoman Teresa Sayward, NY
- Bethany Kosmider, Town of Crown Point Supervisor
- Karen Hennessy, LCBC
- Other members of the LCBC and the Community

☐ Poem by Jean A. Breed: "Golden Gate"

☐ Closing Remarks

☐ Gathering in the Pavilion

Aren't We Lucky

Even though we paid a lot, in money and in pain,
We didn't get to choose this path, but we're lucky just the same.

How many people get to see what's right before our eyes?
During our lives we all can witness the arch reach for the sky.

From one dear bridge we all remember to a new one come to call.
Every single one of us can watch it and see it all.

We slide across on a ferry now and see new stuff every day.
They're building us a brand new bridge to help us on our way.

We all take pictures so we will remember what took place here this fall.
All of us will long remember and look back and recall.

Each day brings some stronger ties to hold it all together.
In years to come we all will cross no matter what the weather.

We'll tell our stories – we each have one – of how we got through this.
Just what we did and just what happened – we all could make a list.

Each day brings a little more peace, our valley is gathering around.
We pray together for that happy day when our new bridge is found.

So take a step back and look at all this and let yourself be amazed.
Aren't we lucky to be alive now and living in this place?

Golden Gate

A year has gone by in this valley; a year since our lives changed.
It's been a long and winding road; we had our lives rearranged.

The simple tasks of everyday that we took so for granted;
Just vanished that October day, like someone moved the planet.

We mourned our loss – our gracious bridge – now just a memory.
We all moved on, we helped each other, that's what we did, you see.

We all spoke out, we beat the drum, and we worked for what we needed.
We didn't give up, not one of us, not till we succeeded.

We drove a thousand miles to work, the businesses took a hit.
But we supported one another, good people just don't quit.

The money for this brand-new bridge seemed so far out of reach.
How the money finally came is a lesson we all could teach.

Our representatives played a part; the coalition was the golden link.
We worked together – all of us – two states are really one, I think.

Now workers have come from far away to build a brand-new span.
I watch them as I cross the lake, and pray God will hold their hand.

We're waiting for the day the bridge will be in place again.
And while we wait we all go on and hold each other's hand.

The businesses have tried to recover; the workers commute each day.
We'll get through this next year all together; we all will find our way.

Golden Gate
(continued)

The people on the ferry get us back and forth each day.
Blessings on those hard-working folks, they help us find the way.

So bow your heads and be so grateful, we're all still here to wait.
One day we'll drive on a brand-new bridge, our own little Golden Gate.

So many people are under so much stress right now, we just need to let it go.

Let it Go

© Jean Arleen Breed

We need some time, we need some space, and we need to let it go.
To start to heal will take a while before the scars don't show.

Remember what we can't forget and push away the rest.
We never thought we would have to fight to pass this horrid test.

One month, then two, then three add up before the journey back.
Regroup and rest, then start again, this time we will attack.

Our eyes are open, now we know, the truth is often gone.
We must remember the ancient words, "It's darkest before the dawn."

Together we have made this trip from here to hell and back.
Together we can start again, and get our life on track.

We have a place that has been blessed, and it's still here for us.
Our home, our job, our business now can flourish from the dust.

So – a few more weeks, a month or two, and then we turn around.
We put one foot and then another and how we will rebound.

Glass

© Jean Arleen Breed

Every day we juggle things, they're all up in the air.
Every day it seems there's more, how did they get there?

Some of them are made of rubber; if we drop them, that's ok.
But some of them are fragile things, once broken they go away.

The trick to all of this, you see, is to know which one is which.
Look at each one carefully before we start to pitch.

We know the bridge was made of glass, it shattered when it fell.
We know the jobs the people held are fragile, we can tell.

The places we know and love so dearly were on that horrid list.
If they close the doors of these great places; they smash it with a fist.

Our valley has been hit so hard, first one, then two, then three.
The juggler surely doesn't know how much this means to me.

Everyone who lives here has been juggling for so long.
We know these things will smash to bits if we all don't stay so strong.

So keep on going and find the strength to not let this all pass.
Don't let the juggler close it all, this valley made of glass.

The Flatiron Construction Company of Colorado was awarded the $69 million contract to build the new bridge at Crown Point. They are starting to arrive from Colorado and there will be a reception where the Lake Champlain Bridge Coalition will give out the packets welcoming the workers. This poem was in the package.

Welcome

© Jean Arleen Breed

Welcome to our valley; we're glad that you could come.
We need some help to build a bridge, and you can get that done.

We've been through hell and back again but now we have such hope,
Now you've come to make it better, to help us all to cope.

We want to make you feel at home, and make this job a safe one.
While you build a bridge for us, we'll pray for you – each one.

May you be blessed in every way as all the weeks go by.
Be careful when you go to work, do your best, just try.

You can see the empty place where our old bridge had been.
That bridge was here for eighty years; before this all began.

We shed a tear when that bridge went, we thought it was a friend.
The closing down, the blowing up – it had a bitter end.

The ferry that we have right now is getting us across.
But there's not one who lives near here who doesn't feel the loss.

So – we look forward to that new bridge; we need it in that space,
It's in your hands to make it work; to fill that hollow space.

We'll cheer you on and help you out and watch as time goes by.
Thanks a lot for coming here – God bless you, and now, goodbye.

Wait

Waiting is so hard to do, it takes a heavy toll.
We all want things to happen now; we want to reach our goal.

Remember those who had to wait for centuries long ago.
They prayed and waited and had such faith, they knew the sky would glow.

The three wise men had to wait to know the time was right.
They traveled to see a miracle, one cold and starry night.

Look how long Noah waited for the water to go down.
He knew the day would finally come when none of them would drown.

Moses waited patiently to get the words we needed.
All the people then found out, the words had best be heeded.

He finished on the seventh day, and on that day, He rested.
He waited until His work was done, and then stood back and blessed it.

So, waiting is a skill we need, from long ago to now.
Just bow your head and say a prayer and take a little vow.

I'll bow my head as I stand there, waiting on the banks.
One day that goal will be right here and then I will give thanks.

March 20, 2010

There wasn't money to maintain our bridge (and ninety-three other failing bridges in New York State), but the State of New York has the money to maintain twenty-seven golf courses!!!

Dear Editor:

State-Owned Golf Courses

During these tough economic times, when people are struggling to justify their jobs at the Moriah Shock, when state historic sites/campgrounds are closing, when the entire Champlain Valley has been put in a horrible position due to the closure/destruction of the Lake Champlain Bridge, I was absolutely disgusted to learn that New York State owns twenty-seven golf courses.

The state owns Bethpage Black Golf Course in Nassau County. This is where many huge PGA Tournaments are played. Imagine how much it would save the state to put all of the courses back in private hands? If the state sold these twenty-seven golf courses, imagine how many people could keep their jobs and how many campgrounds/state historic sites could stay open.

The jobs that all the people so desperately need, and the state historic sites that we should all be entitled to visit, seem much more important than New York State owning golf courses.

I shudder to think what it costs the taxpayers of New York State for these twenty-seven golf courses!

Best regards,

Jean Arleen Breed
Crown Point, NY 12928

Why?

Where did all the values go? What happened to common sense?
Shuffle dollars like dominos. That budget is just pretense!

Take the money for bridge repair and putt it all away.
Is a golf course more important than your family is today?

I don't know just how much it costs to keep those greens all mowed.
I do know that the bridge fell down, we watched it just explode.

Do we need to start all over? It's such a mess right now!
I know we'll make it to the end, but I can't see just how.

Why do we need to justify those jobs that we all need?
The prison guards work hard each day, they all have families to feed.

Maybe all the budgets need a scrutiny line by line.
I know you pay your share of taxes just like I pay mine.

I would hope the money would go to keep this valley safe.
What I hope and what is real doesn't seem to be the case.

So we move on and take each day and speak out when we can.
I'll just keep writing all my letters, I bought a brand new pen!

And Still

No matter what we've done right here, the days keep going on.
Another sunrise shines through the trees, another chance for dawn.

The birds forgive us and keep on singing, the trees somehow survive.
The stream still travels along its path, the forest is still alive.

It's not like it was before we came, then all was a garden to see.
Everything was in its place, the animals all believed.

We managed this and managed that and managed to make a mess.
Just leave the earth alone, my friend, don't help it with your stress.

It had a system that worked just fine, before we took it over.
It knew just how to let things happen, those were the days of clover.

But even though we stomp about and always want our fill.
The good planet earth keeps going on, and I pray it always will.

December 12, 2010

In recent conversations with Cindy—owner of Frenchman's Restaurant in Crown Point—and Lisa—owner of The Bridge Restaurant in Vermont—they both said EXACTLY the same thing to me. They are hanging on by a thread—business is worse than it was at this time last year and they are not sure if they are going to make it. I felt I had to do something; thus the letter.

Dear Editor:

Support Our Local Businesses—on both sides of the lake . . .

Last year, at this time, all of us in the Champlain Valley were struggling to cope with the loss of the Champlain Bridge. The daunting task of getting support and funding to replace this bridge was taken on by many of our small business owners.

When others questioned even rebuilding a bridge near Crown Point, these people fought long and hard to keep everything here where the old bridge stood. I truly doubt we would have the new bridge being constructed now without the heroic efforts of these business owners. They worked so hard, traveled to Albany and Montpelier, and beat the drum long and loud so the rest of us could benefit.

Even though they were hurt so much by the bridge closure, they showed such grace under pressure. One business even opened their door at 4:00 every morning and gave FREE coffee and snacks to all of the travelers who had to drive two hours each morning and two hours each night. These people are truly a credit to our valley, and now they are struggling to survive. A restaurant on the Vermont side gave away FREE coffee and snacks for a long time, and now they too are struggling to make ends meet and stay in business.

In recent conversations with several folks who own local businesses, it seems their business is very slow right now. These people have put everything they have into their business. They work incredibly long hours, have invested their life savings, have contributed tax money to our valley, have kept people employed, and have tried to stay in business until the new bridge is in place and our valley returns to the life that we had.

Some of these folks are barely hanging on and it would be a tragedy to lose them. They survived all that time when they were on "the road to nowhere," and are just trying to survive now.

We must rally around these businesses and support them as they supported us during our darkest hour. They worked incredibly hard to make the new bridge happen and can't turn our backs on them now. It would be tragic if we lost these wonderful people as owners of our businesses and had more empty stores and restaurants.

There are great places to eat, great places to stay, (some wonderful Bed & Breakfast places!), great places to shop, and historical places to see in the Champlain Valley. Please show your encouragement and support to these hard-working people and help them survive. Thank you!

Best regards,

Jean Arleen Breed
Crown Point, NY 12928

Jarrett Elethorp, Jean Arleen Breed, and Dalton T. Elethorp at the Crown Point Lighthouse (photo courtesy of Francis Breed)

Freedom

Long ago, when our country started, folks struggled to survive.
They depended on their own hard work, just to stay alive.

Life was tough and times were hard but they fought for all they had.
They just dug in and kept on working – together it wasn't so bad.

They traveled far and fought a war to survive in this new land.
Every single one of them agreed to take a stand.

"We all came here for freedom and freedom we will have.
We'll fight and win and then sit down and write on our behalf."

Those words they wrote still ring today, we all know them by heart.
These brave first ones just gave their all and gave us all a start.

That same spirit is alive and well; we're free to make our choice.
If there are things that just aren't right, we speak out with one voice.

The ones who rallied around our bridge, the ones who watched it fall.
Speak with that same determined heart; with echoes we recall.

Life should be a happy path; they wrote that in there too.
All the freedoms that they won were passed to me and you.

So as we battle to win our war, remember their rough start.
Be thankful that we have our freedom; and keep it in your heart.

Shine

© Jean Arleen Breed

Who left that light on, I wondered today.
Who left that light on, to show us the way?

It shone on a fort, carved out of stone.
It shone on a lake, so close to my home.

It sparkled on a lighthouse that had stood there so long.
It traveled a great distance just before dawn.

It pointed to the stars with their own magic light.
It beckoned to the moon that lit up the night.

It helped all the spirits who travel at night.
It guided them softly on their nocturnal flight.

It felt like an old friend, one I knew from before.
It had an echo from old days on these rugged old shores.

It helped those before us and the ones before them.
It has been here forever, long before men.

It started with one star that shone in the east.
It continued through all time, through centuries at least.

It will be there forever, long after our time.
It will search for the future, that wonderful shine.

Echoes

As we all stood there and smiled that day, I thought I heard a sound.
A sound that came from long ago echoed all around.

Waves were crashing on the shore; the fog was thick that day.
The light they needed shone from above, and sent them on their way.

For many years the lighthouse worked to keep boats safe from harm.
The narrows was a dangerous place and they needed that alarm.

Eight strong columns held it together and a light was on the top.
When strong winds blew and danger came, that light just never stopped.

The stairs all swirl around in circles and lead right to the sky.
Yes, the trip is worth the climb, just look and you'll know why.

Carl and Auguste created some art to make that lighthouse glow.
If you want to see how magic looks, their works will let you know.

The lighthouse was built, and then built again, and dedicated one more time.
Through all of this, it stood there so proudly, that monument is yours and mine.

No matter what was swirling around, that lighthouse stood right there.
That lighthouse is a special friend; it's here for us to share.

When my sister—who lives in Chicago—comes to visit me, we always go to the forts. She cried when I told her they blew up the bridge. She said it must have been like an execution.

Yes, it was. After all that bridge did for us for almost eighty years, that was its end, and it was indeed very sad.

A walk by the fort is just what we need. To take no special path, just go where they lead.

Jean Arleen Breed and Janice Maas at the Crown Point Forts (photo courtesy of Greg Maas)

The Forts

© Jean Arleen Breed

Chimney Point and His Majesty's Fort surround this ancient place.
Green Mountain Boys and the American Navy – they all left a trace.

The tap of drums, a bugle call, and a soft voice filled the air.
Was that a soldier sitting there? Just sitting on that stair?

The British and the French lived here; they came to defend the land.
The Continental Army came; they too would lend a hand.

The echo from an old-time bugle seemed to pass us by.
A pastor read his words aloud and he was asking, "Why?"

All the ones who were already here joined in for the war.
They showed the ways of the ancient ones, the ones who came before.

I thought I saw a campfire burning way up on the hill.
I turned around and looked that way, but everything was still.

The heavy stones were put in place to build the forts right here.
I thought I heard a hammer fall. I thought I saw a spear.

The ones who came here long ago left so much behind.
The shores have footprints from all the ones whose treasures we still find.

So as we stood there and smiled that day and marveled at this place,
We weren't alone; there were other ones, the ones who left their trace.

Wander

© Jean Arleen Breed

To just take the time to wander along,
To listen to nothing but the earth's sweet song.

To feel the soft sun and smell the pine trees,
This is enough to bring me to my knees.

The lake just shimmers on a day like this.
The birds seem to know that this day is bliss.

The smell of the lilacs is so welcome today.
It brings back sweet memories that I hope will stay.

The lake is so quiet, it seems to be resting.
There's no battle today, nothing is testing.

A walk by the fort is just what we need.
To take no special path, just go where they lead.

An echo of laughter is heard in the distance.
This day is a blessing, I don't doubt His existence.

Let everything rest, let our spirits just smile.
It's been a long time since we've seen this mile.

We're thankful for this day, we needed this rest.
There are too many days when we take the test.

So take some deep breaths and let your cares go.
Go wander today – take everything slow.

The ones that came before us left this just in case we should need it. Cannon overlooking the Crown Point Bridge (photo courtesy Jean Arleen Breed).

Valley Thunder

© Jean Arleen Breed

The thunder of the lofty cannon roared upon the shore.
So many battles were fought right here and now there was one more.

The ones who fought here long ago had left this place for us.
Now our battle loomed ahead and we must keep that trust.

We didn't have that army here – our army was kind of small.
But the courage and the heart they had took it to the wall.

Suddenly we're cut in half with people on both shores.
The bridge that stood here all those years – she had lost her war.

Our enemy wasn't in the hills or hidden down below.
Our enemy was scattered wide and we must charm our foes.

We must find the magic words that bring us back together.
Lucky for us, there were special ones who fought in all the weather.

They didn't ride the hills at night; they rode a bus so far.
They took the battle right to the hill where all the leaders are.

So we didn't need the cannon now but it was good to see.
It reminded us all of other wars – just like our war could be.

So someday if you look out here, you'll see what we see now.
A brand new lady standing there – and now you know just how.

Goodbye, Dear Bridge

© Jean Arleen Breed

The bridge was there for all my life, so solid and secure.
That it would be gone – just blown up – never did occur.

It was so gracious and serene; sometimes it looked enchanted.
I crossed that bridge every day and just took it all for granted.

Not many bridges go uphill and then go down again.
That bridge was such a special one; I felt it was a friend.

For eighty years the bridge had stood no matter what the weather.
I always got to the other side; we survived the storms together.

Then one day, just like that, the bridge was falling down.
Nobody took care of the poor old bridge, no good guys were around.

The money for the bridge repair was spent for other things.
It didn't seem to matter much what the consequences bring.

So now the pieces of the bridge get fished out of the lake.
Millions of dollars will be spent – whatever it will take.

A new bridge will be built right there for all of us to use.
I thank the Lord the poor old bridge didn't make any tragic news.

I'm sure the new bridge will be fine, whenever it gets there.
It just won't have the special feel, the old bridge used to care.

I will remember that gracious one, the one that fell apart.
It will always have a special place right here in my heart.

The Journey

© Jean Arleen Breed

The journey that we've all been on has put us to the test.
All that's happened these last two years just wouldn't let us rest.

The end of our bridge came so quickly, we could barely say goodbye.
The life we knew on these two shores just stopped – and we knew why.

Without a bridge to span the lake the life we lived was gone.
Drive way around the lake each day and that trip took so long.

We didn't sit here and wait to be rescued; we spoke up with one voice.
The business owners and all of us knew we really had no choice.

This valley needed a brand-new bridge, and we needed a ferry for now.
Folks got to work and beat the drum and took a "must win" vow.

The farmers and the little store owners and all of us joined in.
Survival here was what was at stake; we knew we had to win.

They got on buses and went to Albany, and went to Montpelier, too.
Our elected officials heard the words; they knew what they should do.

Two states that really have one heart, two Governors came here to call.
Our little valley must be joined again; apart, both sides would fall.

So plans were made and money spent and soon the ferry came.
Those blessed boats that made the difference; they helped to ease our pain.

The time went by and work was done by folks from far away.
We prayed for them and watched it all until this glorious day.

The Journey

(continued)

A brand-new bridge that spans the lake and heals that broken place.
We all remember our dear old bridge; it stood there with such grace.

Now all of us can drive over the lake and once again be free.
To go to work and go to school or just drive to see the leaves.

That broken place is whole again, our lives have turned around.
From this day on, we all can go wherever our hearts desire is found.

So thank you all that played a part that brought us here today.
Our hearts are filled with hope again and I just have to say,

To all the ones who made this happen, we thank you from the heart.
This journey has been long and painful, but now – again – we start.

The new Lake Champlain Bridge is scheduled to open in late 2011. We begin again . . .

A two-day celebration to mark the opening of the new Champlain Bridge is being planned for this fall. The bridge currently under construction between Crown Point and Chimney Point, Vermont is slated to open in October.

The Lake Champlain Bridge Coalition, a grass-roots group of local leaders and community members, formed the Lake Champlain Bridge Community to create, plan, and direct public festivities that will celebrate the replacement and reopening of the Champlain Bridge.

Bridge Community Co-Chairs are Karen Hennessey and Lorraine Franklin— founding members of the Lake Champlain Bridge Coalition.

"We all look forward to the day the second Lake Champlain Bridge is open."

(Lohr McKinstry – *Press Republican*)

About the Author

A lifelong resident of the Champlain Valley in New York, Jean Breed worked in Vermont for the past thirty years. During those three decades, she drove over the Lake Champlain Bridge more than fourteen thousand times!

New York Congresswoman Teresa Sayward and Vermont Representative Diane Lanpher told Jean that her poems and Letters to the Editor were part of the history of our valley from the time we lost our bridge and they should be saved for posterity. This is part of the reason Jean wrote this little book.

Lake Champlain Bridge Coalition Co-Chair Lorraine Franklin asked Jean to write a special poem to be read at the dedication of the new bridge. Lorraine said: "Your poems touch all of us, and put into words what so many of us can't. It would be fitting that one of your poems would bring us full circle." Jean will read "The Journey"—the last poem in this book—at the opening ceremony for the new bridge.

This is Jean's first book. She hopes to release a second book, *Poems from the Champlain Valley*, before Christmas 2011.